Psychological Manipulation

Ivan Salvaterra

Anuket Publishing

Content

Chapter 1
The basics
of manipulation

If you are alone, then you are completely yours. If there is at least one person next to you, then you belong only half or even less...

Leonardo da Vinci

Psychological manipulation is a complex phenomenon that has intrigued researchers and practitioners for decades. From the times of the ancient Greek philosophers to modern studies in social psychology and cognitive neuroscience, humanity has sought to understand how and why people can be influenced to act in certain ways, even against their interests.

Nobody likes to be controlled. It usurps our ability to act using free will, to perceive the world as we see it ourselves, and to freely choose our values, beliefs, and actions without hindrance. On the other hand, if behavioral control never existed, the world would become chaos. So how can we distinguish constructive control from destructive control?

Each of us has repeatedly encountered other people's actions aimed at controlling our behavior, emotions, or even beliefs. Some of these actions, for example, affectionate correction of a young child's behavior or emotional reactions from loving parents, are quite appropriate and beneficial for personality development.

Destructive forms of psychological control also include attempts by authoritarian and totalitarian states, political parties, religious sects, and criminal communities to control people's beliefs for their selfish purposes.

What is psychological control?

Psychological control (psychological intrusion) is a type of mechanism for manipulating other people's emotions and beliefs for one's purposes. Manipulation is a way to covertly influence a person through indirect, deceptive, insulting, or aggressive tactics. In general, manipulation can affect not only the spiritual sphere but also behavior. In this case, it is a form of behavioral control. Behavior control is necessary at a certain stage of children's education by parents, but it becomes inappropriate in relationships between adults and mature individuals, moving into the category of destructive behavior.

Parental education and control

Normal behavioral control in the parenting process is expressed in the parents' efforts to normalize, regulate, and control the child's behavior. This behavioral control is a natural buffering factor to prevent emotional distress and behavioral problems in children who, due to their age or developmental characteristics, are not able to comply with the norms and rules of life in society, since They don't always know exactly how to behave or how to react to certain life situations. Such parental supervision is appropriate if it takes into account the age and is exercised with respect for the autonomy and personal limits of the child, in the context of showing emotional warmth and sincere participation in the interests and problems of the child.

On the other hand, inadequate parental psychological control can be associated with the development of emotional problems in children, adolescents, and adults. This maladaptive parental control manifests itself in the form of multivariate manipulation strategies and, in most cases, is directed against the autonomy of children in growth and development, for example:

• Emotional blackmail: "If you don't do it, I won't talk to you"
• Imposing feelings of guilt: "Mom became seriously ill after giving birth to you"
• Overwhelming imposition: "Mommy loves you very much."
• Rejection of love: "Come, otherwise your mother will not love you."

Inadequate psychological control negatively affects children, repressing them emotionally, altering their ability to establish emotional connections with other people, and significantly limiting the development of their identity and autonomy. Children raised in conditions of strict psychological control have low self-esteem, and emotional regulation problems, and are more likely than others to suffer depressive episodes.

Roots in Social Psychology

One of the fundamental pillars in understanding psychological manipulation is social psychology. This branch of psychology focuses on how people think, feel, and behave in social contexts. Concepts such as conformity, obedience, social power, and interpersonal influence are fundamental to understanding how manipulation is exercised.

For example, Milgram's famous experiment on obedience to authority revealed how people can obey orders to inflict pain on others simply because of pressure from an authority figure. Similarly, Asch's conformity studies demonstrated how people can give in to group pressure and adopt beliefs or behaviors that differ from their convictions.

Principles of Cognitive Psychology

Cognitive psychology, on the other hand, focuses on how we process information, make decisions, and perceive the world around us. This area of study is essential to understanding why certain manipulation techniques are effective and how they exploit cognitive biases and limitations of the human mind.

Cognitive biases, such as confirmation, availability, and anchoring bias, influence how we interpret information and make decisions. Skilled manipulators can take advantage of these biases to direct our perceptions and decisions toward their own goals.

Differentiating persuasion from manipulation

Persuasion and manipulation are two concepts that are often confused. While both aim to influence the decisions or behaviors of others, the difference lies in the intention and method used.

Persuasion:

• Seeks to convince through rational arguments, information, and evidence.

• It is based on respect for the autonomy and freedom of choice of the other.

• Aim for mutual benefit or at least not seeking to harm the other person.

Examples:

• A salesperson who presents the advantages of a product without resorting to pressure or deception.

• A teacher who uses clear examples and explanations so that her students understand a topic.

• A politician who presents proposals based on data and solid arguments.

Handling:

• Seeks to control or exploit through emotional techniques, deception, or pressure.

• Does not respect the autonomy of the other person and seeks to benefit at their expense.

• It can have negative consequences for the victim, such as emotional, economic, or even physical harm.

Examples:

• A scammer who uses lies and tricks to obtain money from the victim.

• A partner who uses guilt or emotional blackmail to control the other.
• Un líder que utiliza la propaganda y la desinformación para manipular a la opinión pública.

How do we differentiate them?

Persuasion is based on reason, the manipulation of emotion.

Persuasion seeks mutual benefit, manipulation seeks unilateral benefit.

Persuasion respects the autonomy of the other, manipulation nullifies it.

In summary:

• To persuade is to convince with reasons.
• To manipulate is to control emotions.
• It is important to be aware of these differences to avoid being a victim of manipulation and to act ethically and respectfully when influencing others.

Remember:

• It's not always easy to identify tampering, but it's important to watch for the signs.
• If you feel pressured, coerced, or deceived, it is likely that you are being a victim of manipulation.
• If you think you are being manipulated, seek help from a professional or a person you trust.

Brainwashing: when manipulation erodes identity

Brainwashing, also known as coercive persuasion, is a complex psychological process that seeks to control and modify an individual's beliefs, values, and behaviors. It is based on manipulation techniques that weaken identity and the ability to think critically, creating a dependency on the manipulator.

How does brainwashing work?

Brainwashing techniques are usually systematic and gradual, and can be divided into four phases:

1. Weakening: The aim is to isolate the person from their social and family environment, depriving them of support and external points of reference. A state of vulnerability is generated through sensory deprivation, physical or psychological abuse, or humiliation.

2. Induction: The new ideology is introduced repetitively and constantly, using techniques such as propaganda, indoctrination, and coercion. The emotions and basic needs of the individual are appealed to to create a bond of dependency with the manipulator.

3. Exploitation: The person is pressured to renounce their beliefs and values and adopt those of the manipulative group. Total obedience is required and you are punished for any deviation from the norm.

4. Reintegration: The aim is for the person to internalize the new ideology and defend it as their own. You are encouraged to participate in proselytizing activities and recruit others to the group.

Relationship between brainwashing and manipulation

Brainwashing is an extreme form of manipulation, but it is not limited to extreme situations such as cults or totalitarian regimes. Manipulation can be present in any type of relationship, and is characterized by:

Control: The manipulator seeks to have control over the other person's information, decisions, and emotions.

Exploitation: The other person is used for personal benefits, regardless of their well-being.

Misinformation: Reality is distorted to confuse and control the other person.

How to protect yourself from this type of manipulation?

To protect yourself from manipulation it is important:

Be aware of the signs: Be wary of people who try to control you, isolate you, or make you feel guilty.

Maintain a support network: Surround yourself with people who love and support you.

Think critically: Do not accept information without analyzing it and contrasting it with other sources.

Develop self-esteem: Trust in yourself and your ability to make decisions.

Brainwashing is an extreme form of manipulation that can have serious consequences for the mental health and identity of the victim. It is important to be aware of signs of manipulation and develop tools to protect yourself.

The Role of Historical and Contemporary Examples

To illustrate these concepts, it is useful to examine historical and contemporary examples of psychological manipulation. From propaganda campaigns during World War II to manipulative marketing strategies in the digital age, these cases provide a window into how individuals and institutions have used manipulation throughout history to influence the masses.

Historical examples:

Ancient Rome: Roman emperors used bread and circuses to keep the masses happy. They offered free food and public shows to distract the population from political and social problems.

Witch trials: In the 16th and 17th centuries, thousands of women were accused of witchcraft in Europe and North America. These accusations were often the product of personal grudges or rivalries, and women were tortured until they confessed.

Nazi Propaganda: The Nazi regime systematically used propaganda to manipulate the German population. They used messages of fear, hatred, and nationalism to convince people to support the war and the persecution of the Jews.

Milgram Experiment: In 1963, Stanley Milgram experimented to study obedience to authority. Participants in the experiment believed they were administering electric shocks to another person, but in reality, the shocks were fake. The experiment showed that people are willing to obey authority even when it orders them to do things they believe are wrong.

Contemporary examples:

Marketing: Companies use marketing techniques to influence their purchasing decisions. They use subliminal messages, misleading advertising, and other techniques to convince us to buy products we don't need.

Social networks: Social networks can be used to manipulate our opinions and beliefs. Social media algorithms show us content that confirms our biases and isolate us from information that might challenge them.

Fake news: Fake news is false or misleading information that is deliberately spread. Fake news can be used to manipulate public opinion and sow discord.

Chapter 2
Persuasive influence techniques

Basic techniques and tactics of non-professional (domestic) handlers.

All manipulators (domestic and professional) maintain their power over people through targeted manipulation, abuse, and coercive psychological control, both continuous and periodic. By maintaining control to do what they want, manipulators strive to:

• Avoid escalating the conflict and bringing it to light.
• Put the other person on the defensive instead of attacking the manipulator.
• Make the victim doubt himself, his abilities, qualities, and abilities.
• Hides his selfish or aggressive intentions.
• Avoid personal responsibility.
• Avoid the need to change anything.

As a result of manipulation, the other becomes a victim and may lose confidence in himself, in his feelings and perceptions, which allows the manipulator to control him.

Manipulation techniques can include overt aggression such as intimidation, threats, insults, humiliation, criticism, narcissistic abuse, subtle forms of emotional abuse, physical abuse, and punishment.

Veiled techniques include condemnation, accusation, complaining, comparisons, scolding, tutoring, persuasion and arguing, lying, silence, simulation, inducing self-pity, feigning ignorance, playing helpless, crying, complaining, denying, bullying, gossiping, and rumors. ridicule, humor, witticisms, sarcasm, labels, contempt, blackmail, sabotage, bribes, flattery, gifts and favors, seduction and sex, intellectualization and "speaking openly", assumptions and provocative questions, provocations, emotional blackmail, evasions, forgetfulness, delays, inattention, false concern, sympathy, apologies.

Many of these behaviors are not inherently harmful and are even appropriate in certain circumstances. What determines whether a person is manipulative or not is not determined by the behavior itself but by the context in which the behavior is used and the intention behind the action or words. An intention becomes manipulative when it is driven by a hidden and unstated desire that is designed to deceive another person and influence their perceptions, beliefs, emotions, and ultimately force them to take or refuse to take some action.

The ability to persuade others to adopt certain beliefs, attitudes, or behaviors is a powerful skill used in a variety of contexts, from advertising and marketing to politics and personal relationships. Persuasive influence techniques are key tools in the arsenal of communicators and leaders, and understanding how they work can be invaluable in a world where persuasion is ubiquitous.

1. Establishing Credibility:

A fundamental technique of persuasive influence is establishing credibility. People tend to be more receptive to messages from those they perceive as experts, authorities, or trustworthy people on the topic at hand. Therefore, the communicator must present his or her argument convincingly, supported by solid evidence and relevant credentials.

2. Appeal to Emotion:

Another powerful technique is to appeal to the emotions of the target audience. Emotions such as fear, happiness, sadness, or anger can significantly influence people's decisions and actions. Persuasive communicators use emotional stories, powerful images, and evocative metaphors to emotionally connect with their audience and motivate them to act in a certain way.

3. Creation of Scarcity and Urgency:

Creating scarcity and urgency is a technique commonly used in sales and marketing. By presenting an offer as limited in time or quantity, you increase the perception of value and motivate people to take quick action to seize the opportunity before it disappears. This technique activates the psychological principle of aversive loss, where people value what they could lose more than what they could gain.

4. Use of Reciprocity:

Reciprocity is a powerful psychological principle that states that people tend to return favors and acts of kindness. Persuasive communicators can take advantage of this principle by offering something of value for free or by making a generous gesture before asking for something in return. This creates a sense of obligation and increases the likelihood that the person will respond positively to the request.

5. Consistency and Commitment:

People tend to act in ways consistent with their prior commitments and self-perceived identities. Persuasive communicators can take advantage of this principle by getting people to publicly commit to a specific idea, goal, or action. Once a person commits verbally or in writing, they are more likely to follow through with that commitment to remain consistent with their self-image.

6. Presentation of Social Evidence:

Presenting social evidence involves showing people that others, especially those who are similar to them, have adopted certain beliefs or behaviors. This phenomenon is based on the principle that people tend to follow the example of those they perceive as similar or who are in a similar situation. Testimonials, reviews, and case studies are effective ways to use social evidence to influence people's attitudes and behaviors.

Manipulation techniques

These are the most common manipulation techniques:

1. Gaslighting:

It is a form of psychological manipulation in which the manipulator seeks to make the victim doubt their perception of reality. He does this by denying facts, distorting information, or outright lying.

Example: A manipulative person may deny having said something they did say, or may accuse the victim of imagining things.

2. Gaslight:

Similar to gaslighting, gaslighting seeks to disorient the victim and make them feel unsafe. The manipulator uses sarcastic comments, insults, or ridicule to undermine the victim's self-esteem.

Example: A manipulative person may make comments about the victim's appearance, intelligence, or abilities.

3. Projection:

The manipulator attributes his or her thoughts, feelings, or actions to the victim. This may be a way of denying one's negative behavior or making the victim feel guilty.

Example: A manipulative person who is unfaithful may accuse the victim of being unfaithful.

4. Triangulation:

The manipulator involves a third person in the relationship to create tension or conflict. This may be a way to control the victim or isolate them from their loved ones.

Example: A manipulative person may speak badly about the victim to her friends or family.

5. Silent treatment:

The manipulator stops talking or communicating with the victim as a form of punishment or control. This can be very painful and confusing for the victim.

Example: A manipulative person may stop talking to the victim for days or even weeks.

6. Blame:

The manipulator makes the victim feel guilty for her feelings or actions. This may be a way to control the victim or avoid responsibility.

Example: A manipulative person may blame the victim for her aggressive behavior.

7. Amortization:

The manipulator gives small favors or gifts to the victim to compensate for her negative behavior. This may be a way to manipulate the victim into staying in the relationship or into forgiving the victim's behavior.

Example: A manipulative person who has been unfaithful may buy the victim flowers as a way of asking for forgiveness.

It is important to remember that these are just some of the most common manipulation techniques. Manipulators can use a variety of techniques to control and exploit their victims.

If you believe you are being a victim of manipulation, it is important to seek professional help. A therapist can help you identify manipulation techniques that are being used against you and develop strategies to protect yourself.

Persuasion techniques in advertising

Advertising's main objective is to influence consumer behavior, and to do so it uses a series of persuasion techniques. Some of the most common are:

1. The emotional appeal:

Humor: A funny ad can be more memorable and effective than a serious one.

Fear: Ads that appeal to fear can be very persuasive, especially if the fear is of something the consumer already has.

Positive feelings: Ads that create positive feelings, such as happiness or nostalgia, can also be very persuasive.

2. Social proof:

Testimonials: Ads featuring testimonials from satisfied customers can be very persuasive.

Endorsements: Advertisements that feature celebrities or experts endorsing the product can also be persuasive.

Figures and statistics: Using data to show that the product is popular or effective can be an effective form of persuasion.

3. Scarcity and urgency:

Limited-time offers: Creating a sense of urgency can motivate the consumer to purchase the product immediately.

Limited editions: Offering a product in a limited edition can increase its appeal.

Discounts and promotions: Offering a discount or promotion can be an effective way to persuade the consumer to buy the product.

4. Reciprocity:

Gifts: Offering a gift in exchange for purchasing a product can be an effective form of persuasion.

Free samples: Offering a free sample of the product can convince the consumer to buy it.

Free trials: Offering a free trial of the product can be an effective way to persuade the consumer to purchase it.

5. Authority:

Experts: Using an expert to endorse the product can be an effective form of persuasion.

Celebrities: Using a celebrity to promote the product can be an effective form of persuasion.

Institutions: Using the logo of a recognized institution can increase the credibility of the product.

It is important to be aware of the persuasion techniques used in advertising to make more informed purchasing decisions.

Tips to avoid being persuaded by advertising:

Don't get carried away by emotions. Analyze the product or service rationally before purchasing it.

Research the product or service before purchasing it. Read reviews from other consumers and compare prices.

Don't let yourself be pressured by a sense of urgency. If you are not sure whether you want to buy a product, wait until you have more time to think about it.

Be critical of the information presented in advertising. Don't believe everything you read or hear.

Advertising can be a useful tool for consumers, but it is important to be aware of the persuasion techniques used to make informed purchasing decisions.

Persuasion techniques in politics

Persuasion is a fundamental element in politics. Politicians use various techniques to influence public opinion and gain the support of citizens.

Persuasion techniques

Rational arguments: Politicians use rational arguments to convince citizens that their ideas are the best. They present data, statistics, and examples to support their arguments.

Emotions: Politicians also appeal to citizens' emotions to generate support. They use inspiring stories, emotional images, and language that awakens feelings such as fear, hope, or anger.

Credibility: Politicians try to build their credibility so that citizens trust them. They present themselves as honest, competent, and experienced people.

Repetition: Politicians repeat their key messages over and over so that citizens remember and associate them with them.

Simplification: Politicians simplify complex problems so that citizens understand them easily. They often use slogans and short phrases that are easy to remember.

Testimonials: Politicians use testimonials from influential people or ordinary citizens to support their ideas.

Humor: Humor can be an effective tool to connect with citizens and make your messages more memorable.

Examples of persuasion techniques in politics:

A politician who uses data and statistics to prove that his economic plan will create jobs.

A candidate who uses a moving personal story to connect with voters.

A political leader who presents himself as a protector of the people.

A political party that uses a simple and catchy slogan for its campaign.

A celebrity who supports a particular candidate.

A politician who uses humor to criticize his opponent.

It is important to be aware of the persuasion techniques that politicians use to critically evaluate their messages. We must not get carried away by emotions or by the simple repetition of a message.

Tips for critically evaluating persuasive messages:

Pay attention to the arguments that are presented. Are they rational and fact-based?

Consider the source of the message. Is someone credible and trustworthy?

Analyze the language that is used. Does it appeal to emotions or fear?
Compare the message with other sources of information. Are there other perspectives that are not being considered?

Think by yourself. Don't let yourself be carried away by social pressure or the opinion of the majority.

Being a critical citizen is essential for a healthy democracy. By being aware of persuasion techniques and critically evaluating political messages, we can make informed and responsible decisions.

Manipulation or persuasion techniques using NLP

Neurolinguistic Programming (NLP) is a set of techniques based on the idea that our thoughts, emotions and behaviors are shaped by our language and our sensory experience.

1. Anchor
2. Modeling
3. Use of Language
4. Calibration

Language plays a crucial role in persuasion. By using specific words and phrases, it is possible to influence people's beliefs and emotions. NLP suggests using positive, solution-oriented language to create an effective impact.

Example: A life coach uses positive and motivating affirmations during a session with his client. Instead of saying, "You can't afford to make mistakes," she says, "You can learn and grow from every experience, even mistakes." This approach encourages the client and empowers them to face challenges with a positive mindset.

NLP techniques for persuasion:

Rapport: It is the creation of a connection and trust with the other person. It can be achieved by synchronizing posture, tone of voice, and breathing rate.

Calibration: Calibration involves observing and recognizing subtle changes in a person's body language, voice, and facial expressions to adapt your communication approach and maintain connection. By paying attention to non-verbal cues, you can adjust your message to maximize its impact.

Example: During a negotiation, a businessman notices that his counterpart frowns slightly when certain terms are mentioned. Instead of insisting on those points, he adapts his approach and presents alternatives that generate a more positive response from the other party.

Anchors: They can be used to create positive or negative emotions in the other person. Anchoring is a technique that associates a stimulus with a specific emotional response. It consists of linking an intense emotional experience with an external stimulus, such as a gesture, a word, or an image. Once anchoring is established, the stimulus can activate the desired emotional response.

Example: A salesperson wants to create a positive association with his product in the customer's mind. During the presentation, every time the customer expresses interest or emotion, the salesperson subtly touches the customer's shoulder. Over time, the salesperson's simple touch will activate the customer's sense of interest and excitement, increasing the chances of a sale.

Milton Model: It is a set of language patterns that are used to create ambiguity and uncertainty in the other person. This can make her more susceptible to persuasion.

Metamodel questions: These are questions used to obtain information about how the other person thinks and feels.

Reframing: It is the reinterpretation of a situation or event more positively or favorably.

Examples of NLP techniques in everyday life:

A salesperson who uses rapport to create a connection with a potential customer.

A teacher who uses calibration to observe the learning needs of his students.

A therapist who uses anchors to help a patient overcome a phobia.

A lawyer who uses the Milton Model to create doubt in a jury.
A manager uses metamodel questions to understand an employee's motivations.

A politician who uses reframing to present an unpopular policy in a more positive light.

It is important to note that NLP is not a magical tool. It cannot be used to control people or make them do something they do not want to do. However, it can be a useful tool to improve communication, persuasion, and influence.

Tips for using NLP ethically

Use NLP to create positive and trusting relationships.

Respect the autonomy and freedom of choice of other people.

Don't use NLP to manipulate or exploit other people.

Be honest and transparent in your intentions.

NLP can be a powerful tool for good or evil. It is important to use it responsibly and ethically.

Chapter 3
Handling
in personal relationships

Personal relationships are the connective tissue of our lives, providing emotional support, companionship, and a sense of belonging. However, sometimes these relationships can be marred by the presence of manipulation, a phenomenon that can erode trust, undermine self-esteem, and distort relational dynamics. In this chapter, we will explore how manipulation manifests itself in personal relationships and how we can address this challenge.

Identifying Manipulation

Manipulation in personal relationships can take many forms, from subtle tactics to more direct strategies. Some common examples include using guilt to get what you want, emotional manipulation to control your partner, or using victimization to gain sympathy and attention.

Destructive psychological control as a form of manipulation

If someone begins to control your beliefs, emotions, and behavior, then they are simply stealing part of your Being. In fact, by obediently succumbing to the manipulation of your parents, boss, or the "talking head" on television, you cease to be yourself with all your originality. Start trying to change your true sincere feelings, and your true beliefs for those that are beneficial to others. Even if you convince yourself at the level of consciousness that "black" is "white", then at the subconscious level a conflict will mature in your soul between the need to think one thing, say another, and feel a third. Due to internal conflicts, psychosomatic disorders (peptic ulcer, hypertension) may occur, and you may begin to suffer from shame, guilt, self-denial, and decreased self-esteem. If you see or feel that you are in such a relationship, know that you are being manipulated and controlled.

Examples of manipulation and psychological control

Feeling controlled by another person can be one of the worst feelings in life. Every person by nature has the right to freedom of feelings, emotions, and beliefs. Control limits our ability to explore the world around us, develop and grow in our way, make our own decisions, and learn from their consequences. Inadequate psychological control can destroy relationships (personal and professional), destroy trust, and lead to passive defensive or active aggressive reactions. This is true not only at the level of interpersonal relations but also at the level of relations between society and state institutions.

The appropriate control needed (both on a personal and social level) must be balanced with respect for personal boundaries and autonomy, compassion, understanding, and patience. Without these things, the necessary psychological and behavioral control becomes a dictatorship that turns people into slaves. Feelings of insecurity, low self-esteem, imposed feelings of guilt, the need to constantly make excuses, and mental confusion are emotional markers of destructive personal, business, or social relationships in which they manipulate you and try to control you.

Why do people try to control it?

This is what usually causes some people to control the behavior of others:

• Your feelings of helplessness and insignificance,
• The desire to turn other people's actions for your benefit.
• Try to hide your defects.
• Tries to evade responsibility, the need to act,
• The desire to get rid of their anxieties, which they cannot cope with on their own.
• Hoping to ensure that they will never be abandoned or rejected.
• Deep-seated fears of not being attractive to oneself or others.

Signs of psychological control in private, commercial, and public relationships.

A controlling person or organization often exaggerates the seriousness of the situation and uses words like "always" or "never" to describe themselves or others:

"You never loved me!", "I always went out of my way for you!" , "International Politics: The situation is very tense!

The controller bribes with praise, favors, help, or gifts: "You have so much talent!"

The manipulative person bombards you with expectations, rules, or desires. This is often the most difficult type of psychological control. Any meeting with such a person can seem like hard work, in which it is necessary to meet expectations and not cause disappointment: "Honey, you are the ideal man that I have dreamed of all my life!", "If I behave well, you will do it". Take me to Bali?", "You must be the best (beautiful, rich, cool)", "Don't you want to disappoint us?"

The manipulator takes care of you like a child, first of all, controlling where you are and what you are doing. If you feel uncomfortable from constant and intrusive monitoring, then this is no longer a worry, but an attempt to control you.

A person who controls others appeals to basic fears (emotional, physical, and financial) with his words and actions: "Do you want to be left alone?", "Do you want to be left without money, without a job and friends?", "Do you want to be left alone?" What do you want in Paris?", "This is for your safety."

A controlling person constantly reminds you of his ultimate importance, asserting a position of power and dominance in the relationship. "You learn from me",

"The eggs don't teach the chicken", "If not me, who?", "This is no place to argue!"

A controlling person does not allow responding on the substance during discussions, cutting you off, repressing you, and "mocking" you: "What will be your positive decision?", "Okay, quickly sign here and here", "No. Let's discuss!", "If grandmother were grandfather..."

A controlling person tries to lower the other's self-esteem and provoke a feeling of guilt: "You ruined my life!", "Who are you?", "What have you done for the country?"

A controlling person pits family members, employees, social groups, or other groups of people against each other, using vile motives: "Gutierrez, he's going to trade in his second car in a year!"

A controlling person usually appeals to absolute values. Strict religious or moral and ethical norms are used to induce feelings of guilt: "You are a believer!", "You are a communist!", "Leave your pride and show proper humility!"

A controlling person refuses to admit blame for his actions and mistakes, transferring it to others: "You ruined my life!", "It starts with yourself," "It's all the machinations of the State Department!"

When interacting with a controlling person, one feels used, intimidated, guilty, and ashamed.

A controlling person is only kind and accommodating to you when he wants something in return.

Power and Control Dynamics

Manipulation in relationships is often based on power and control dynamics. The manipulator may attempt to exert control over the other person by limiting their autonomy, restricting their freedom, or manipulating their emotions. This can create a power imbalance in the relationship, where one party has unfair control over the other.

Social manipulation

Emotional manipulation is a process in which a person attempts to influence or control the emotions, thoughts, or behaviors of another person to gain an advantage or achieve their own goals. It can manifest itself in a variety of ways and often involves the use of subtle or deceptive tactics.

Some examples of emotional manipulation include:

Guilt and Victimization: The manipulator can make the other person feel guilty or responsible for something, even when they are not. This can lead the victim to act according to the manipulator's wishes.

Intimidation and Threats: The manipulator may use fear or intimidation to control the other person. This may include verbal or physical threats.

Mind Games: The manipulator may play with the victim's emotions, such as making them feel insecure, jealous, or confused. This can weaken the victim's self-esteem and confidence.

Seduction and Charm: Some manipulators use their charm or attractiveness to gain the other person's trust and then manipulate them.

Silence and Withdrawal of Effect: The manipulator may ignore or withdraw affection as a form of punishment or control. This may cause the victim to seek approval or make concessions to regain attention.

It is important to recognize the signs of emotional manipulation and set healthy boundaries in relationships to protect yourself against this type of behavior.

Typology of Manipulative People

Everett Leo Shostrom, a psychologist and interpersonal communication expert, developed a typology of manipulative people that focuses on how they use different influence strategies to control others. According to Shostrom, these are the main types of manipulators:

The seducer: This type of manipulator uses charm, flattery, and persuasion to influence others. They are experts at making people feel special and desired, which makes them more receptive to your desires and demands.

The pleaser: Clingy, is a manipulative person who exaggerates his dependence, weakness, and inability. This is a person who wants to force others to care about him. The benefit is to shift worries onto someone else's shoulders. Subtypes of the clingy manipulator: Parasite, Complainer, Eternal Child, Hypochondriac, Dependent, Helpless, Suffering, Unhappy. Complacent manipulators seek to please others to get what they want. They are helpful and attentive, but their apparent generosity can be a tactic to manipulate others into doing what they want.

The bully: A bully is a manipulator who uses exaggerated aggression, cruelty, and ill will to control other people. He controls with the help of various types of threats. Hooligan-Manipulator Subtypes: Insultor, Hater, Gangster, Threatener, Grumpy Woman. They can be physically or emotionally intimidating, making people afraid to challenge their desires.

The Dictator: a person who exaggerates his strengths and capabilities for himself and others, dominates and orders control of his victims, and does not tolerate objections or insubordination. There are stable subtypes of Dictator: Leader, boss, Preacher, and God's Helper.

The Rationalizer: Calculator, exaggerates the need to constantly keep everything and everyone under his control. He treats everyone and everything with distrust, always trying to check everything. He knows better than others that people can deceive, because he, above all, deceives, evades, and lies. Typical subtypes of this manipulator: are businessman, scammer, gambler, advertiser, and blackmailer. This type of manipulator uses logic and reason to justify his actions and convince others to do what he wants. They may distort the truth or manipulate information to support their arguments and persuade others.

The sufferer: The most common couple with the Dictator is usually his victim and a complete antipode. He is often found in family tandems manipulating each other. The one who considers himself a "rag" exaggerates his sensitivity and passivity, showing characteristic techniques: forgetfulness, passivity, silence, and demonstrating low self-esteem. Subspecies of the "rag": suspicious, stupid, chameleon-like, conformist, confused, withdrawn. Suffering manipulators victimize themselves to gain sympathy and attention from others. They may exaggerate their problems or difficulties to manipulate others into helping them or making concessions on their behalf.

The good guy: is a person who exaggerates his affection, love, and attention. If the Dictator uses evil to control others, the Nice Guy uses good to control others. Dealing with him is usually more difficult because the Nice Guy's manipulative intentions are not on the surface, and it is much more difficult to catch him in manipulation. Interestingly, in any conflict between a bully and a good guy, the bully loses. Manipulator subtypes: Companion, Virtuous Moralist, Representative of the public, or representative of the organization.

The judge: He is a person obsessed with criticism. He doesn't trust anything or anyone, he always looks for evil, accuses, gets indignant, and doesn't know how to forgive. Manipulator subtypes: Omniscient, Accuser, Verifier, Evidence Collector. Appraiser, avenger, forced to admit guilt.

The Defender: he is the exact opposite of the Judge. A person who wins over others with his support, concern for the needs of others, and patience when making mistakes. He gains control by not giving people the opportunity to develop their independence, making people need him constantly. Manipulator subtypes: Savior, Sugar Daddy, Mother Hen with Chicks, Comforter, Patron, Martyr, Helper, Selfless.

These categories provide insight into how different types of manipulators employ various strategies to achieve their goals. Recognizing these patterns can help people protect themselves from manipulation and establish healthy boundaries in their interpersonal relationships.

Handler profiles

In general, three profiles of manipulators are the most common: the narcissist, the psychopath, and the controller. It is important to understand that these are just examples and that there are many other types of manipulators.

1. The narcissist:

Narcissists are people with a great sense of grandiosity and a constant need for admiration. They tend to be very charming and charismatic, but they can also be very demanding and exploitative. They often manipulate people to get what they want, whether it's attention, recognition, or power.

Characteristics of the narcissist:

Inflated sense of importance
Need for admiration
Lack of empathy
Exploitation of relationships
Grandiosity
Arrogance

2. The psychopath:

Psychopaths are people who lack empathy and remorse. They are often very intelligent and charming, but they can also be very dangerous. They manipulate people to get what they want, regardless of the harm they may cause.

Psychopath characteristics:

Superficial charm
Lack of empathy
Impulsiveness
Pathological lies
Handling
criminal conduct

3. The controller:

Controllers are people who need to be in control of everything and everyone. They are often very insecure and jealous. They manipulate people to manage them and can be very possessive and abusive.

Controller Features:

Need for control
Unsafety
Jealousy
possessiveness
emotional abuse

It is important to remember that not all manipulators fit perfectly into these profiles. Some manipulators may display characteristics of two or more types. The important thing is to be aware of the signs of manipulation and take steps to protect yourself.

Tips to protect yourself from manipulators

Set clear boundaries.
Don't be intimidated.
Trust your instinct.
Talk to someone you trust.
If you feel threatened, seek professional help.

If you think you are being a victim of manipulation, you are not alone. Many people have been through the same thing and there are resources available to help you.

Main types of manipulative influence schemes.

E. Shostrom identifies four main types of manipulative systems:

1.   An active manipulator tries to control others through active methods, never showing weakness. This is a person who always dominates interactions, taking advantage of others' lack of strength, knowledge, or skills. He uses his social or official position, and his rank for selfish purposes, defeating the enemy: this is a father, a security officer, an official, a sergeant major, a teacher, a boss, and a superior. The technique used: is "obligations and expectations", the principle of the rank table. The main philosophy of an active manipulator is to dominate at all costs.

2. A passive manipulator presents himself as a helpless, inept, and insufficiently intelligent person. Achieve the desired control not through victories, but through defeats. When combined with an active manipulator, the passive wins, allowing the active manipulator to think and work for him. Lethargy and passivity are the main weapons of such a manipulator. Passive roles of manipulators: student, beginner, muslin miss, sick, unfortunate, injured, etc. The philosophy of a passive manipulator is to never irritate.

3. The competitive manipulator constantly plays or fights with others, perceiving people as rivals or enemies, real or potential. He can use both active and passive techniques. The philosophy of a competitive manipulator is to win at any cost.

4. An indifferent manipulator plays on indifference and disinterest, declaring his main catchphrase "I don't care." He can use passive or active tactics, playing the Grumpy Woman or the Martyr of Love. The most typical manipulation game is the "Threat of Divorce" to retain the partner. But a threat is always an attempt to control a person, and not a desire to carry out the threat itself, from which the manipulator himself will lose. The philosophy of the indifferent manipulator is to reject care.

Impact on Self-Esteem and Confidence

Manipulation can have a devastating impact on the self-esteem and confidence of the person being manipulated. Manipulative tactics can make a person feel insecure, helpless, or doubtful of themselves. Over time, this can erode his sense of self-worth and his ability to trust his judgments and decisions.

Cycles of Manipulation and Abuse

In some cases, manipulation in relationships can evolve into more serious forms of emotional, verbal, or even physical abuse. Cycles of manipulation and abuse can trap the person in a pattern of harmful behavior, where the manipulator exerts control over them and then manipulates them to stay in the relationship.

Addressing Manipulation in Relationships

Addressing manipulation in personal relationships can be challenging, but it is a crucial step in restoring the health and integrity of the relationship. Communicating openly and honestly about manipulative behaviors, setting clear boundaries, and seeking outside support are important steps in addressing this issue.

To prevent manipulation in personal relationships, it is essential to cultivate relationships based on mutual respect, trust, and open communication. Fostering empathy, understanding, and commitment to the well-being of others can strengthen the bond between people and create a healthy and balanced relational environment.

Manipulation in personal relationships is a complex and harmful phenomenon that can undermine the health and happiness of the people involved. Recognizing the signs of manipulation, setting clear boundaries, and seeking help when necessary are important steps in addressing this issue and cultivating healthy, rewarding personal relationships.

Chapter 4
Handling
in the media

Politics and the media play a crucial role in forming opinions, attitudes, and perceptions in society. However, behind the appearance of objectivity and neutrality, an insidious phenomenon often hides: manipulation. In this chapter, we will explore how manipulation manifests itself in these areas. social.

Psychological manipulation in politics

Although the goal of political manipulation is ultimately the same as commercial advertising, the difference is that in politics, in exchange for your money, you do not receive a specific product or service (in politics it is most often being sold unrealistic promises and hopes), even if this contradicts your true desires and aspirations.

Falling under psychological control, most unprepared people react in a way that is completely expected and beneficial for the manipulator: they feel guilty, feel unimportant, begin to doubt themselves, lose autonomy and personal boundaries, and experience negative emotions. towards themselves or others, show external aggression, or react unacceptably.

Important! Experiencing negative emotions after communicating with a person, a group of people, or contacting the media is the most important marker (red flag) that you have been subjected to hidden or overt manipulation, that is, an attempt to control you. against his own will and beliefs.

However, understanding the essence of manipulation, its mechanisms and the true goals of the people who control you will give you the strength to remain yourself and live your own life in your interests, and not for the sake of "peace." world".

Who usually manipulates you?

At home, in the family, among loved ones and friends, at work, or school, unprofessional manipulators often try to control you: people with certain heightened personality traits, who have experienced psychological trauma that ultimately led to the formation of a pathological system of its psychological defense: through the control that surrounds people, achieving power and dominance, as a means of protection against their deepest fears and chronic anxiety, their low self-esteem and their destroyed self-identity.

In most cases, these are people with personality disorders: borderline personality, narcissistic, sociopath, psychopathic, asocial. These people can use both conscious and unconscious manipulation tactics, which they developed as a means of adaptation and survival in the unfavorable conditions in which they lived. For example, manipulators often include children from single-parent families, orphans, children in orphanages, prisoners, members of criminal communities, religious sects, law enforcement officers, drug addicts and alcoholics, and businessmen. Often, such people are distinguished by a passive-aggressive style of manipulation, when anger and hostility are expressed in hidden, indirect and conditionally acceptable ways:

Examples of passive aggression in speech.

In public life, psychological manipulations are on a larger scale and are organized by professionals - "engineers of human souls": psychologists, psychiatrists, journalists and publicists, bloggers, influencers and trolls, directors, advertising specialists, public relations, ministers of all kinds: cults, politics, intelligence services. Manipulation is a psychological weapon (psychological warfare) to wage psychological wars in the real and virtual world. An extremist form of psychological weapon is terrorism: its goal is to change the behavior of entire states and societies for their purposes. On a psychological level, this is also manipulation.

Professional psychological manipulation in advertising and politics

Psychological manipulations in the media, public, and political life are carried out by true professionals in their field. The problem of bad manipulation in advertising or politics usually lies in the fact that the "engineers of human souls" themselves are under manipulative pressure from clients and politicians, which leads to counterproductive interaction between top officials and politicians. artists.

Professional advertising and political propaganda use a combination of rational and emotional persuasion (the persuasion spectrum). Manipulative influence on the audience (society) usually begins with less rational persuasion (essentially coercion), which are measures capable of influencing the majority of society, which are less sophisticated in education, cognitive skills, and knowledge of psychology with a gradual transition to rational persuasion directed at the intellectual and most persistent elite of society.

Threats and emotional violence are rarely used in advertising but are quite common in the political propaganda of totalitarian states. In advertising and propaganda of non-aggressive states, manipulation, and rational persuasion are most often used.

The ultimate goal of all types of advertising is to persuade the consumer to purchase a product or service. In politics, the most common thing is that an unknown future is sold in exchange for the present. Manipulative advertising achieves its objectives by using facts and arguments that deceive and manipulate the emotions of consumers or voters: exaggeration of the quality of a product or problem solved by a politician with false arguments.

Emotional appeals

The first type of manipulative advertising and propaganda is misleading advertising, which uses false facts. Uses confusing and misleading statements when promoting a product or policy. The facts provided are usually secondary or frankly false. Important facts are often hidden and not mentioned. For example, the advertisement mentions that the product does not contain substances harmful to the environment, something that everyone hears. These products never contained these substances, but they have other environmental disadvantages that they prefer to keep silent about.

The second type of advertising or manipulative propaganda is based on false arguments, allowing errors in reasoning. For example, advertising "traditionally made" products based on "ancient recipes", which is practically impossible in the modern conditions of the food industry.

The third type is an appeal in advertising or propaganda to emotions rather than logic. This advertising or propaganda is directed not only at the conscious level but also at the subconscious. Advertisements may include appeals to the need to achieve, to dominate, to feel secure, to satisfy curiosity, the need for sex, appeal to the herd instinct, the need to belong, orientation, fame, attention, autonomy, the need for food, drink, sleep, etc. They can also use fear to take advantage of panic if necessary. These techniques are often used in drug advertising and political advertising, exploiting fear of the future, of strangers, and of the unknown. Advertisers and propagandists play with consumer emotions, linking a product or policy with happiness, health, security, success, and friendship in the future, family, home, etc.

The opposite of manipulative advertising is honest advertising, which provides objective information about a product, service, or policy, uses credible reasoning, and allows people to make their own informed decisions. both in the purchase of goods and services and in the political future of their country.

The nature of Media Manipulation:

Manipulation in the media can take many forms, from the selection of information to the distortion of the truth and the creation of biased narratives. The media can influence public opinion by choosing which stories to cover, how to present them, and which angles to highlight, all to shape public perceptions.

Disinformation and Propaganda

One of the most worrying aspects of media manipulation is the spread of misinformation and propaganda. Through the dissemination of false or misleading information, the media can influence people's beliefs and behaviors, undermining democracy and trust in institutions.

Biases and Agenda Setting

Implicit and explicit biases in the media can also contribute to manipulation. Journalists and editors may have their own ideological or political leanings that are reflected in the selection and presentation of news. Furthermore, the phenomenon of "agenda setting" dictates which issues are considered important by the media, thus influencing the public's concerns and priorities.

Media Manipulation Strategies

Within the field of media manipulation, there are several common strategies and tactics used to influence public perceptions. These may include the use of shocking images, emotionally charged language, repetition of key messages, and the creation of stereotypes or caricatures of certain groups or individuals.

Social and Political Consequences

Manipulation in the media can have profound social and political consequences. It can polarize society, fuel hatred and division, and erode trust in democratic institutions. Furthermore, it can perpetuate stigmas and prejudices, undermining inclusion and equality in society.

Addressing Media Manipulation

Addressing manipulation in the media requires a multifaceted approach involving the media, regulators, the public, and society as a whole. It is essential to promote media literacy to enable people to discern between truthful information and misinformation. Additionally, greater transparency and accountability are needed in the media industry to ensure integrity and objectivity in news coverage.

Manipulation in the media is a complex and multifaceted phenomenon that can have significant consequences for society. Recognizing and addressing manipulation in the media is crucial to preserving the integrity of information and protecting the health of democracy.

Manipulation in politics: A Puppet game

Politics, that intricate world where the decisions that impact our lives are woven are not always governed by transparency and honest debate. In the shadows, a dark puppet master hides manipulation.

What is political manipulation?

It is the use of strategies to influence public opinion, emotions, and the behavior of citizens, to obtain a political benefit. It is about weaving a web of lies, half-truths, and emotions to control the masses as if they were puppets.

The most common techniques

Propaganda: Misrepresenting information, exaggerating achievements, and hiding deficiencies to create a false image of a candidate or party.

Fear: Instilling fear through real or imagined threats to get people to vote for a candidate or support a cause.

Disinformation: spreading false or misleading information to confuse the population and delegitimize opponents.

Personal attacks: discrediting rivals with insults, slander, and rumors to divert attention from their shortcomings.

Populism: appealing to the emotions and prejudices of the people, promising easy solutions to complex problems.

Why is political manipulation dangerous?

It erodes trust in democratic institutions, weakens citizen participation, and creates a climate of polarization and hatred. In the worst case, it can lead to the seizure of power by authoritarian or extremist leaders.

How to combat political manipulation?

Develop critical thinking: analyze information objectively, look for reliable sources, and verify data before sharing it.

Promote media education: teach people to discern between true and false information, and to identify manipulation techniques in the media.

Demand transparency: pressure politicians and parties to be honest and accountable for their actions.

Strengthen democratic institutions: defend freedom of expression, access to information, and the right to political participation.

The fight against political manipulation is a collective responsibility. Only through education, active participation and the demand for transparency can we prevent puppets from taking control of the political scene.

Chapter 5
The ethics of manipulation

Manipulation is a pervasive phenomenon in human life, present in a variety of contexts, from advertising and marketing to politics and personal relationships. However, the question of whether manipulation is ethical or not is a topic of debate that raises fundamental questions about power, autonomy, and moral responsibility.

Manipulation is a "toxic" form of psychological exploitation of other people, when the manipulator, using hidden, indirect, deceptive, abusive, or aggressive tactics, achieves the desired changes in the actions, behaviors, perceptions, emotions, and beliefs of others.

All types of manipulation have two main objectives: To gain influence and provoke certain actions or inactions of the victims to satisfy their selfish objectives, and to gain power and control over people.

In this chapter, we will explore the ethical complexities surrounding manipulation and how we can approach this challenge thoughtfully and ethically.

The positive side of manipulation

The word "manipulation" has a negative connotation, and rightly so. It is often associated with control, exploitation, and deception. However, manipulation is not always a bad thing. There are some situations where manipulation can be beneficial.

Examples of the positive side of manipulation:

Motivation: A coach can use manipulation to motivate his players to give their best effort. For example, he can tell them that they are the best or that they have the potential to win the championship.

Persuasion: A salesperson can use manipulation to persuade a potential customer to buy a product. For example, he may use the scarcity principle by saying that there are only a few units available.

Education: A teacher can use manipulation to keep his students' attention. For example, he can use games or interactive activities.

Therapy: A therapist may use manipulation to help a patient overcome a problem. For example, she may use the empty chair technique to have the patient dialogue with her past self.

It is important to note that manipulation is only positive when used ethically and responsibly. If it is used to control, exploit, or deceive other people, then it is negative.

Tips for using manipulation positively:

• Be honest and transparent in your intentions.
• Respect the autonomy and freedom of choice of other people.

• Use manipulation to create positive, trusting relationships.
• Do not use manipulation for personal gain at the expense of others.
• Manipulation is a powerful tool that can be used for good or evil. It is important to use it responsibly and ethically.

Avoid personal responsibility for your actions or inactions.

Manipulators are found in our lives wherever we gather: at home, on the playground, at school, at university, at work, in churches, in stores, in the media, and on the Internet. Above all, there are many manipulators in public and political life, in the form of propaganda and advertising, both commercial and social, as political and psychological combat operations.

The very essence of politics is the manipulation of people's consciousness to achieve in society certain beliefs, emotions, and behavioral reactions that are beneficial to the ruling or dominant group, or the autocrat or dictator, that political manipulators use to achieve their personal selfish goals. Political manipulation, propaganda, and "brainwashing" are often masked by the scientific euphemism "social engineering."

Defining Manipulation and Ethics:

Before we dive into the ethics of manipulation, it is important to define our terms. Manipulation refers to subtle or deceptive influence that seeks to control or direct the behavior, beliefs, or emotions of others to satisfy the manipulator's interests. Ethics, on the other hand, refers to the moral principles that guide human behavior and determine what is right or wrong, just or unjust.

Ethical Perspectives on Manipulation

From an ethical perspective, manipulation raises a series of moral dilemmas. Some argue that manipulation is inherently wrong because it violates the principle of respect for the autonomy and dignity of others. According to this view, manipulating someone involves treating them as mere means to an end, rather than recognizing their inherent dignity as a human being.

On the other hand, some argue that manipulation can be ethical in certain contexts, as long as it is used to promote the well-being of others or to achieve legitimate and morally justified objectives. According to this perspective, manipulation can be a legitimate tool to influence human behavior and achieve positive results, such as persuading someone to adopt healthier habits or to promote charitable causes.

Ethical Considerations

When evaluating the ethics of manipulation, it is important to consider a number of key factors. These include transparency and honesty in communication, respect for the autonomy and dignity of others, and consideration of the potential negative consequences of manipulation.

Lack of transparency and honesty in manipulation undermines trust and integrity in human relationships, which can have detrimental long-term consequences. Furthermore, manipulating someone without their consent can be seen as a violation of their autonomy and dignity, undermining their ability to make informed decisions and act according to their own values and desires.

Addressing Manipulation Ethically

Addressing manipulation ethically requires a thoughtful approach and awareness of the moral consequences of our actions. This involves being aware of our own motivations and values, as well as considering the impact of our actions on others. Furthermore, it involves practicing empathy and respect towards others, recognizing their dignity and autonomy as human beings.

Ultimately, the ethics of manipulation is a complex issue that requires a careful balance between pursuing our own interests and respecting the rights and dignity of others. By addressing manipulation ethically, we can foster healthier, more authentic relationships based on trust, respect, and integrity.

Chapter 6
Defense against manipulation

Manipulation is a powerful tool used in a variety of contexts to influence the decisions and actions of others. From false advertising to coercive persuasion tactics in personal relationships, manipulation can be difficult to detect and resist. However, there are effective strategies that can be used to protect and defend one's autonomy against manipulation. In this final chapter, we will explore some of these strategies and how they can be implemented in daily life.

Ways to counter manipulation

If you consider yourself a victim of manipulation, don't be discouraged: there are ways to protect yourself in this type of discordant and destructive relationship.

A key component of self-defense is understanding one of the basic premises: psychological manipulation only works one way: if you let it.

Most likely, the handler has studied you and knows your main weaknesses and disadvantages. He knows what you want: to be good, caring, loving, responsible, heroic, patriotic, professional, the best, rich, powerful, etc. Political manipulators know that you want to live in a safe world, be confident in the future, have a roof over your head, and a job, raise your children in peace, and enjoy life. Knowing your desires, strengths, and weaknesses, manipulators will use you to their advantage.

The only way to get out of the standard developmental trajectory of a manipulative relationship is to stop worrying about what the controlling person is trying to convey and instill in you.

Below are some common tactics that can be used to break a manipulator's control or mitigate it:

• Before reacting in any way to an influence that seems manipulative, try to analyze what the person wants to convey to you and what they might want from you. If you don't understand what's happening, take a break and consult with people you trust, or just try to figure it all out in a calm environment, without rush or emotional pressure.

• Stop being defensive. If you start to notice that he is making excuses, simply end the conversation and walk away.

• Date to stop being right and being good. Be yourself, even if you don't live up to other people's expectations. Let them remain "unsatisfied" with your expectations; This is not your business or your life's business.

• Try to fake or give up the desires and needs that got you hooked on the manipulator. Without the bait you swallow, no one can control you. Remember that most promises made by people with personality disorders and politicians are never kept.

• Remember that as soon as you expose the manipulation and get out of the manipulator's control, he will make new attempts and significantly increase the pressure on you. Be prepared for this: the new level of impact on you can be unpleasant and even dangerous.

• Defender in his position. Don't give in to pressure. Most of the time, the manipulator wants to avoid war, not start it.

• Stop trying to change the person who constantly manipulates you. Let him be manipulative if that is his choice. Just accept it as a fact and stop trying to change it. This does not mean that you will obey him or continue communicating with him.

• If you find it difficult to deal with existing problems on your own, you can always seek professional psychological help.

Tools to get out of the clutches of a manipulator

1. Develop critical thinking

One of the most powerful defenses against manipulation is to develop critical thinking. This involves actively questioning the information you receive, evaluating the credibility of sources, and examining arguments with healthy skepticism. Do not accept information passively; Instead, look for evidence, contrast different points of view, and keep an open but analytical mind.

2. Learn to recognize manipulative tactics

Becoming familiar with common manipulation tactics will help you identify them when they occur. Some of these tactics include; threats, fear, shame, or flattery to influence decisions. Pay attention to attempts at emotional pressure, withholding relevant information, or the use of fallacious arguments.

The more aware you are of these tactics, the more able you will be to resist their influence.

3. Set clear boundaries

An important part of defending yourself against manipulation is setting clear boundaries and maintaining them firmly. Communicate our boundaries directly and respectfully, and not be afraid to defend them when challenged. Maintain autonomy and not feel forced to give in to the manipulative demands of others. Remember that you have the right to make your own decisions and act according to your values and needs.

4. Trust your intuition

Intuition can often be your best ally in defending against manipulation. If something doesn't feel right or seems suspicious, trust your instincts and reflect on why you feel that way. Intuition is a powerful tool that can alert you to manipulative situations before you are even able to rationally identify them.

5. Cultivate healthy relationships

Relationships based on trust, mutual respect, and open communication are less prone to manipulation. Cultivate healthy relationships with people who value our autonomy and support our decisions. If you suspect that a relationship is being manipulative or toxic, do not hesitate to seek support from friends, family, or trained professionals.

6. Educate others and promote awareness:

Finally, a powerful way to defend against manipulation is to educate others and promote awareness on this topic. Share knowledge about manipulative tactics and defense strategies with friends, family, and online communities. The more informed people are, the more able they are to recognize and resist manipulation in all its forms.

Defending against manipulation requires a proactive and conscious approach. By developing your critical thinking, recognizing manipulative tactics, setting clear boundaries, and cultivating healthy relationships, you can protect yourself and others from deception and preserve your autonomy and dignity.

How to resist psychological control over your feelings and beliefs.

When you realize that a person is trying to psychologically control you for their own sake, it is important to remember that you have every right to protect yourself from physical, emotional, and mental harm.

You have the right to speak your mind and discuss your own needs, and by default, you deserve respect. While the person trying to control you obviously won't like hearing all of these statements, you must start by establishing and claiming your boundaries and your right to autonomy.

Response to the manipulator: set personal boundaries

Remember that you have every right not to do, feel, or think what the controlling person wants you to do. You have the right not to sacrifice your happiness, well-being, and integrity by not succumbing to their manipulative ways of controlling. By standing up for yourself, and your autonomy, and refusing to submit to controlling behavior, you will even be doing the manipulator a favor, as you can make him or her understand the destructive nature of his or her behavior.

Having recognized the manipulation, first of all, do the following:

Say "no" calmly to what is contrary to your Being. Say "no" to yourself and loudly to someone who is trying to control you.

Talk openly with the controlling person about how he or she makes you feel. However, avoid emotions, judgments, anger, disappointment, or tears. Stay calm and express your feelings. If this doesn't help, consider whether your disappointment in the relationship is worth it and whether you should continue to feel controlled by this person in the future.

Ask the person if they understand that they are trying to manipulate you and what causes them to do so. Without getting into an argument, explain that you don't appreciate his attempts to control you. If you have noble goals (as you think) for his behavior, this has the opposite effect, causing tension in relationships or cooperation.

Be clear about your boundaries, for example: "I will not work for free after hours or on weekends."

Communicate honestly with that person, when you think they are disrespecting you, say so immediately and openly.

Remember that by accepting gifts and services, you show the manipulator that he has the right to exploit.

People who "have your best interests at heart," want to "change you for the better," "make you a person," and control you only because they are struggling with their insecurities, low self-esteem, worry, and anxiety. using hypercontrol as a means of their psychological protection.

Remind yourself and the manipulator that you are not the source of his problems and that he must independently take responsibility for his actions and their consequences, for example: "I am not to blame for your addiction and I will not give you money for it." one dose (bottle). And if you steal money, you will be caught and convicted."

Maintain a healthy emotional distance and avoid interacting with a controlling person (even virtually) if you can.

Avoid manipulative people until you are strong enough to accept their controlling behavior without emotion. If one gets angry or shows any signs of anger, the manipulator will immediately change the situation and blame you: "You are angry (yelling, upset)!"

Openly minimize the person's expectations and desires for you, communicate that he cannot accept your rules and that he cannot be held responsible for what he likes or dislikes.

Maintain strong personal boundaries and be careful what you say to others: don't let them discover your weaknesses. You don't have to tell anyone what you feel, worry, wish, or fear.

When browsing cyberspace, do not get into arguments with aggressive people, do not look at the messages and letters of the person who controls you, and block him on social networks.

If a person speculates about lofty or religious feelings to make him feel guilty, remember that this type of behavior has nothing to do with faith, religion, or love of country. Focus on the truth: Don't let anyone blame you if you have nothing to blame yourself for.

Remember, if a person manipulates or controls you, this already means that he does not love you and treats you without respect, no matter what he says.

Prioritize your own needs and those of others. Try to maintain physical, emotional, and spiritual health to cope with manipulation and psychological control.

Remember that other people are responsible for their happiness, not you.

Join support groups, learn to resist other people's control and manipulation, and seek professional psychological help.

How to overcome the trauma of manipulation

Overcoming the trauma of psychological manipulation is a process that requires time and effort. However, with the right tools and support, it is possible to heal and regain confidence in yourself and others.

Resources that can help you overcome the trauma of manipulation:

Therapy:

Individual or group therapy can help you understand the impact of manipulation on your life, develop

strategies to cope with trauma and strengthen your self-esteem.
Look for a therapist with experience in trauma treatment and psychological manipulation.

Support groups:

Joining a support group can help you connect with others who have gone through similar experiences.

Sharing your story and hearing the experiences of others can help you feel less alone and validate your emotions.

Online resources:

Numerous online resources offer information about psychological manipulation and trauma, as well as tips for recovery.

Some organizations offer online support groups or forums where you can connect with other people.

Tips for Recovery

Practice self-care: It is important to take care of your physical and mental health. Get enough sleep, eat healthy, exercise, and spend time doing activities that make you feel good.

Build your self-esteem: Manipulation can damage your self-esteem. It is important to work on strengthening your self-confidence and your abilities.

Learn to set limits: It is important to learn to establish clear and healthy limits with other people.

Surround yourself with positive people: Surround yourself with people who support you and make you feel good about yourself.

Be patient: Trauma recovery takes time. Don't be discouraged if you don't see immediate results.

Overcoming the trauma of manipulation is a challenging process, but not impossible. With the right help, you can heal and get your life back.

Remember:

You're not alone.
Some people love you and support you.
You deserve to be happy.

#######